D1521280

Pebble®

Manx Cats

by Wendy Perkins

Consulting Editor: Gail Saunders-Smith, PhD

Consultant: Jennifer Zablotny, DVM
Member, American Veterinary Medical Association

Capstone
Mankato, Min

Pebble Books are published by Capstone Press,
151 Good Counsel Drive, P.O. Box 669, Mankato, Minnesota 56002.
www.capstonepress.com

1 2 3 4 5 6 13 12 11 10 09 08

Library of Congress Cataloging-in-Publication Data
Perkins, Wendy.
     Manx cats / by Wendy Perkins.
     p. cm. — (Pebble books. Cats)
     Includes bibliographical references and index.
     ISBN-13: 978-1-4296-1217-3 (hardcover)
     ISBN-10: 1-4296-1217-7 (hardcover)
1. Manx cat — Juvenile literature. I. Title. II. Series.
SF449.M36P47 2008
636.8'22 — dc22   2007017794

Summary: Simple text and photographs present an introduction to the Manx breed,
its growth from kitten to adult, and pet care information.

Note to Parents and Teachers

The Cats set supports national science standards related to life
science. This book describes and illustrates Manx cats. The images
support early readers in understanding the text. The repetition of
words and phrases helps early readers learn new words. This book
also introduces early readers to subject-specific vocabulary words,
which are defined in the Glossary section. Early readers may need
assistance to read some words and to use the Table of Contents,
Glossary, Read More, Internet Sites, and Index sections of the book.

Table of Contents

The Dog Cat

Some people think
Manx cats act like dogs.
They often follow their
owners around and
growl at strange noises.

Many Manx cats
have no tails.
Other Manx can have
short or long tails.

A Manx's front legs are
shorter than its hind legs.
Some Manx cats hop
when they run.

From Kitten to Adult

Manx kittens are curious.
They like to run and play.

A mother Manx cat
calls to her kittens.
Her high, wobbly sound
is called trilling.

14

Adult Manx trill
for their owners
when they want to
be petted or need food.

Caring for Manx

Manx cats can have short or long fur. Owners should brush their Manx often.

Owners need to feed
their Manx every day.
Dry, crunchy food helps
keep a cat's teeth clean.

Most Manx cats like
kids and other cats.
Manx make good pets.

Glossary

curious — eager to explore and learn about new things

growl — a low, deep noise

trill — to make a high, wobbly sound

wobbly — unsteady

Read More

Barnes, Julia. *Pet Cats.* Pet Pals. Milwaukee: Gareth Stevens, 2007.

Loves, June. *Cats.* Pets. Philadelphia: Chelsea Clubhouse, 2004.

Shores, Erika L. *Caring for Your Cat.* First Facts. Positively Pets. Mankato, Minn.: Capstone Press, 2007.

Internet Sites

FactHound offers a safe, fun way to find Internet sites related to this book. All of the sites on FactHound have been researched by our staff.

Here's how:

1. Visit *www.facthound.com*

2. Choose your grade level.

3. Type in this book **ID 1429612177** for age-appropriate sites. You may also browse subjects by clicking on letters, or by clicking on pictures and words.

4. Click on the **Fetch It** button.

FactHound will fetch the best sites for you!   23

Index

Word Count: 133
Grade: 1
Early-Intervention Level: 16

Editorial Credits
Erika L. Shores, editor; Renée T. Doyle, set designer; Veronica Bianchini and Ted Williams, contributing designers; Linda Clavel, photo researcher

Photo Credits
Chanan Photography, 8
Fiona Green, 14, 16, 18, 20
iStockphoto/Sergey Siz`kov, 18 (food)
Jupiterimages, cover, 1, 22
Norvia Behling, 4, 6, 10, 12